He Took My Lickin' for Me

He Took My Lickin' for Me

 A CLASSIC FOLK TALE

Retold by Timothy Robinson

Illustrations by Ben Sowards

SHADOW
MOUNTAIN

Library of Congress Cataloging-in-Publication Data

Robinson, Timothy M., 1967-
  He took my lickin' for me / written by Timothy Robinson ; illustrated by Ben Sowards.
    p.   cm.
  ISBN 1-57008-953-1 (alk. paper)
  1. Corporal punishment—Fiction. 2. Rural schools—Fiction. 3. Virginia—Fiction. I. Sowards, Ben. II. Title.
  PS3618.O338 H4 2003
  813'.6—dc21   2003010573

Printed in China   68875-7070
Palace Press International, Hong Kong

10 9 8 7 6 5 4 3 2 1

This story is not mine.
It is a folk tale that belongs to the ages
and is retold here for those who seek to feel
more deeply the love of Christ. –TR

For my older brother Jesse. Through his
loving example and the many lickings he took for me,
I have come to a more tangible understanding of
the Savior's love for His brothers and sisters. –BS

O nce upon a time, long ago, during the Great Depression, way up in the mountains of Virginia, there was a one-room schoolhouse and a pack of rowdy students that no teacher could handle. The boys were so rough that they had sent four teachers packing that very year.

A young, gray-eyed college graduate answered the ad for a new teacher and was given the job. The old school director looked him up and down and warned him, "I don't want to mislead. You're in for a beatin', ain't no bones about it. Every teacher's took it, and you'll take it, too."

"I'll risk it," said the young man.

The next morning the newly hired teacher stood before the class. "We're here to conduct school," he said. The boys in the class screamed and hooted. One of the boys, Big Tom they called him, leaned over to the others and said, "I won't need no help. I can chase this little bird myself."

"Now I want a good school, but I admit I don't know how to do that without your help.

S uppose we have a few rules. You tell me what rules we should have, and I'll write them on the blackboard."

"No stealin'!" someone shouted, and the teacher wrote it on the board.

"On time!" came another. Soon there were ten rules written out neatly on the board.

"Now a rule is not much good without a punishment attached," said the teacher. "What should we do if someone breaks the rules?"

Ten licks with the rod without his coat on!" someone yelled.

The teacher looked up at the rod hanging on the wall. "Ten licks. That's pretty severe, boys. Are you ready to stand by it?" The class agreed.

N ot long after, Big Tom came into class very upset. Someone had stolen his lunch. The teacher interviewed the boys one by one and soon discovered the thief—a little scrawny fellow, scarcely ten years old.

The teacher called the boy forward to receive his punishment. "Take off your coat," he instructed.

"I deserve it. I'm guilty. I'll take the ten licks, but please don't make me take off my coat."

"Were you here the day we made the rules?"

The boy nodded, and the teacher took the rod down from its hook.

Y ou agreed to live by it. Take off your coat."

"Please don't make me," the boy pleaded. But slowly his fingers began to work at the buttons on his jacket, and what did the teacher see? He had no shirt on underneath, and the bones in his bare back stuck out all over. The boy's face was red with shame.

❧ ❧ ❧ ❧ ❧

W hy have you come to school without your shirt, Jim?" the teacher asked.

"My daddy's dead and my momma's poor. I only got but one shirt, and it's in the wash today. I wore my brother's big coat to keep warm."

The teacher looked down at the rod in his hand. He hesitated, unsure what to do.

Suddenly Big Tom jumped to his feet.

"I'll take his lickin' for him," he said.

"Very well," said the teacher. "There is a certain law that provides for a substitute, if you're all agreed."

Tom ripped off his coat and stood over the other boy. The teacher started the lashings, but after the fifth stroke the rod broke across Tom's back. The whole class was sobbing.

Little Jim had reached up from below and caught Tom with both arms around his neck. "I'm sorry I took your lunch, Tom," he cried. "I was awful hungry. I'll love you forever for takin' my lickin' for me. Yes, I will love you forever."

Surely he hath borne our griefs, and carried our sorrows: yet
we did esteem him stricken, smitten of God, and afflicted.

But he was wounded for our transgressions, he was bruised
for our iniquities: the chastisement of our peace was upon him;
and with his stripes we are healed.

All we like sheep have gone astray; we have turned every one to
his own way; and the Lord hath laid on him the iniquity of us all. . . .

Yet it pleased the Lord to bruise him; he hath put him to grief: when
thou shalt make his soul an offering for sin, he shall see his seed, he shall
prolong his days, and the pleasure of the Lord shall prosper in his hand.

He shall see of the travail of his soul, and shall be satisfied:
by his knowledge shall my righteous servant justify many;
for he shall bear their iniquities.

 Isaiah 53:4–6, 10–11